VINDICATION

BY

WILLIAM HOYT,

OF HIS RIGHT, BY LETTERS PATENT,

As first Inventor of Locomotives for Ascending and Descending Inclined Planes.

In addressing the public on a subject relating to the private affairs of a citizen, it is proper to state the reasons which have induced the writer to trouble his fellow-citizens with the history of his private business. My apology for thus troubling you at this time, fellow-citizens, is, that you have already, through the newspapers of our county, and by rumor, been apprised that a controversy exists between myself and Andrew Cathcart, in relation to the improved plan of constructing locomotives for ascending and descending inclined planes of Railroads, now in successful operation upon the plane of the Madison and Indianapolis Railroad. The point of controversy is. who first invented said improvement, Mr. Cathcart or myself. I wish simply to state the facts in reference to the invention of said improvement, as they stand upon the record, sworn to by respectable citizens of our county, and let the public judge between us whether Mr. C. or myself is entitled to the credit and profit of said improvement.

The facts are, that in the spring of 1840, I made a model of said invention at the Railroad depot at North Madison, which model had not attached to it the movable wheel, adjusted to the unevenness or irregularities of the track, by means of a lever operated upon by weights and springs, as patented by me on the 17th day of April, 1849. Within two weeks after making said model. (as shown by the testimony of James Davidson,) I discovered the necessity of having the cog or pinion wheel that works into the cog rack situate in the centre of the track, movable, so that it could be elevated or depressed, in order that the teeth of the cog or pinion wheel would work into the teeth of the cog rack, nothwithstanding the unevenness of the track. By the unevenness of the track, I mean the elevation or depression of the side rails of the road, above or below the cog rack which is stationary in the centre of the road. Having discovered the principle of the movable wheel, I found that it was necessary to apply lever power to said wheel to keep it constantly in gear with the stationary cog rack; hence it was that I discovered the application of the lever to said movable wheel, operated upon by weights or springs, as hereinafter described. Both these improvements, viz: the movable wheels and the lever operating upon it as first described, were made in the spring of 1840, within two weeks after I had made my first model. I took my model to Baltimore, Philadelphia and Washington city, the same spring for the purpose of inducing men of capital to aid me in procuring a patent and putting the improvement into practical operation, but in this endeavor I failed, and was not able, even to procure a patent for my invention until April, 1849.

In 1840, I filed in the patent office at Washington, specifications for my improvements, thereby giving notice to the world of my discovery.

In the fall of 1844, or spring of 1845, I was introduced to Andrew Cathcart, Esq., a Scotchman, and then foreman in the machine shop of the Railroad Depot, and made known to him my invention. About one year afterwards, I learned that Mr. C. had gone to Philadelphia to construct a locomotive upon the plan of my invention, and had taken with him a model of said invention to deposit in the patent office at Washington City, for the purpose of procuring a patent for the same.

In the spring of 1848, Mr. C. returned from Philadelphia, bringing with him a locomotive constructed upon the plan of my invention, and by a contract with the Railroad company, put said locomotive upon the plane of the Madison and Indianapolis Railroad, where it has been in successful operation ever since.

Said contract is set forth in the deposition of W. N. Jackson, Secretary of said Road, by the terms of which agreement the Company advanced the funds to build said locomotive, and became the purchaser of said improvement, provided it could be brought into successful operation, and that Cathcart would secure them by good and legal letters patent. Upon this subject, particular attention requested to the deposition of Mr. Jackson. Upon examining the locomotive of Mr. C., I found it was constructed upon the same principle of my invention. I immediately notified the Railroad company of this infringement, and forbade the use by any and all persons whatsoever of said invention, as it of right belonged to me as the discoverer. As soon as I laid claim to the invention, the Railroad company and Mr. C. attempted by every means in their power, fair or foul, to prejudice the public against my title to said discovery; indeed they seemed to regard it as the heighth of presumption in an humble individual, struggling hard against poverty, to obtain his daily bread, *to* set up an honest and rightful claim against a rich and usurping corporation that has neither a body to be clothed and fed, nor a soul to be saved.

Notwithstanding the opposition of the Railroad Company, and its emissaries, W. N. Jackson and A. Cathcart, who made a visit to Washington City to prevent the issuing of a patent to me, and to secure one for Cathcart, alias the Madison and Indianapolis Railroad Company. I succeeded in April last, in procuring my patent, the (then) Commissioner, Edmund Burke, Esq., deciding in favor of my application against Cathcart.

One specimen of the fair dealing of Messrs. Jackson & C., I will give to the public. They procured a model similar to the first model which I made in 1840, and took it to the Patent office at Washington, representing it as my improvement, when they knew that I had discovered and actually made upon a second model in the same year and within two weeks after I had completed my first model, the improvements of the movable wheel, by means of weights or springs. Since the issuing of my patent, Mr. C. applied for a patent, claiming to be the original inventor. and the new Commissioner, Mr. Ewbank, under the law prescribing his duty in case of conflicting applications for the same invention, appointed the first Monday of September last, to try and determine who was entitled to the invention by priority of discovery. Mr. Ewbank, our new Commissioner, decided that A. Cathcart was the first inventor of the improvement. The priority of invention is the only question upon which the Commissioner can pass his judgment under the patent laws, and yet Mr. Ewbank decided that C. was entitled to priority of invention, in direct opposition to the sworn statements of James Davidson, Samuel Thomas, James Patton and Enoch D. Withers, all respectable, honest citizens of our own county, and Henry T. Smith and Warren Little, of Washington City, in whose shop I had my model in 1840, with the improvement of the movable wheel and the lever. The only testimony Cathcart had or could produce, showed conclusively that his pretended discovery was not made earlier than the Spring of 1845, or the Fall of 1844. I challenge a denial of this statement, and can and will show by Cathcart's OWN DEPOSITIONS, if it is controverted, that my statement is strictly and literally correct. Mr. C. gave me notice that he would commence taking depositions at the Railroad office in the city of Madison, to be read before the Commissioner of Patents at the hearing of his application for a patent. Accordingly, on the 17th day of August last, we commenced taking depositions on my competitor's own territory, viz: the Railroad office. Why this place was selected by Mr. C. will appear hereafter.

In the centre of the room stood a long table, at its head sat John Brough, Esq., President of the Railroad company, fronting the witnesses that were called upon the stand to depose. On his right sat the Ex-Governor of Oregon, Joseph G. Marshall, Esq., and next to him, M. G. Bright, Esq., both stockholders and directors of the Railroad company, both acting on this occasion as the attorneys of A. Cathcart—having previously protested when notice was attempted to be served upon them by me, as Cathcart's attorney's, (he being absent from home,] that they were not employed by C., but by the Railroad company. Notwithstanding the acknowledged ability and high legal attainments of Messrs. Marshall and Bright, they were not sufficient in the opinion of Cathcart, alias the Railroad company, to manage the case correctly; therefore, Mr. Brough was called in to counsel and advise, and in fact to conduct the examination of the witnesses. One reason, among others, why Mr. Brough aided in the examination of the witnesses was, no doubt, the fact that Cathcart's witnessess being chiefly employees of the Railroad company, and Mr. Brough, as President of the Company, had it in his power to build up or tear down whomsoever he pleased, might, by his presence, influence and give direction to testimony. By the use of the terms, "influence and give direction to testimony," I do not mean to charge any of the witnesses with false swearing. I wish simply to state facts, and let the public judge of results, and deduce conclusions from the premises. The reason for selecting the Railroad office as the place of taking depositions, would have been obvious to any one in the least conversant with the controversy, who was present during the examination of the witnesses. In the building where the Railroad office is located, are a number of rooms which served, on this occasion, the place of ante-rooms. A witness was brought up stairs prior to his examination, ushered into one of those ante-rooms, where he was confronted by Mr. Jackson or the Old Fox (Brough) himself. What occurred within the walls of the ante-rooms, I leave you, fellow-citizens, to judge.

Not having the pecuniary means of the Railroad company, I was not able to employ as many or as experienced counsellors as my opponents, and therefore relied solely upon John A. Hendricks, Esq., a young man, in justice to whom I must say, managed the case to my entire satisfaction. I employed Judge Sullivan to assist Mr. Hendricks in taking depositions, but the Judge having become disgusted, abandoned the case in a few hours in a few hours from the commencement of taking the depositions, because of the course pursued on the part of the President of the Railroad and the other managers, in persisting to direct the answers of the witnesses in their answers to questions. Had it not been for the kindness of my young friend, Mr. H., I would have been left at the mercy of the Philistines.

I will now give such parts of the testimony as are material, and pertinent to the controversy between myself and Mr. Cathcart, alias the Railroad company, and leave my case, for the present, with my fellow-citizens. It will be hereafter left to a jury of my countrymen, at Indianapolis. I would publish the whole testimony on both sides, but for the reason that I am unable to bear the expense.

TESTIMONY.

Part of Samuel Thomas' Deposition.

Question 3d, *by Hoyt*—State when Hoyt first disclosed to you his invention—his description of the same, and, generally, all you know about it—and whether the drawing here presented you, marked exhibit "A" with the name of Gam'l Taylor there under written, is a correct description of said improvement, so far as the movable wheel, bridge-trees, lever and springs, or weights are concerned.

Ans.—To the best of my knowledge it was in the spring or summer of 1840, Hoyt made a model at the shop of the Railroad company, at North Madison, of a Locomotive, embracing the track and wheel, on which there were two cog wheels. These wheels were both stationary; one wheel was on the axle of the driving wheel which works into a larger wheel, which wheel was on a separate shaft other than the axle of the driving wheel, and worked into a rack in the centre of the track. After he had said model made, he discovered it would not answer. He then stated to me that he had discovered another way, and that was the spur wheel that geared into the rack, which was to accommodate itself to the unevenness of the track by means of a movable bridge tree attached to a lever, which lever pressed the spur-wheel into the rack. I believe the drawing here presented, marked exhibit "A" so far as the movable wheel, bridge tree and lever are concerned, is correct.

Q. 4, *by same.*--You say that after Hoyt had made his model in the spring or summer of 1840, that he made an improvement upon it. State how long it was after said model was made?

ANS.—It was within a month.

Q. 5, *by same.*—What is your business or occupation? How long have you been engaged in said business? Were you ever employed by the Madison and Indianapolis Railroad company, and how long were you employed by said company?

ANS.—I am a machinist, and have been engaged in said business some twenty years, I was engaged in building locomotives several years. I was employed by the company of the Madison and Indianapolis Railroad and by the State some six or seven years. I was superintendent of machinery while in said employ.

Q. 6th.--Did you help Hoyt make his first model to which you have referred? and state if you are aware of the fact why Hoyt did not put his improvement in said model?

ANS.—I helped Hoyt make his first model; I done some turning for him; he wanted to make some improvements, and I advised him not to do it until he would go to Philadelphia and see Mr. Baldwin. Baldwin is an engine builder. I suppose this is the reason he did not put his improvement on said model.

JAMES DAVIDSON—of lawful age and sound mind—being produced and sworn, deposes and says:

QUESTION 1st.—*By Hoyt's Attorney*—How long have you been acquainted with William Hoyt—where does he reside, and what is his business or occupation?

ANSWER.—I have been acquainted with William Hoyt about twenty years—he now resides in Dupont, in Jefferson county, in Indiana—generally occupied in mechanical operations, getting out patents, &c.

Q. 2d.—Where do you reside—and what is your occupation?

Ans.—I reside in Jefferson county, Ind.—I have resided in said county for thirty-five years, last past—the first part of my life, I followed the business of millwright, say for ten years, since then I have lived on a farm, and engaged in running mills.

Q. 3d.—Is the trade or business of a millwright of such a nature as necessarily to acquaint one following that business intimately with the structure and operation of machinery?

Ans.—I think it is.

Q. 4th.—Did Mr. Hoyt ever disclose to you the fact that he had discovered and invented an improved plan for the construction of Locomotives, for ascending and descending inclined planes on Railroads? If so, state the time when he made the disclosure, and his explanations of his invention or improvement.

Ans.—He did make a disclosure to me of his improvement. The first of his models he showed to me was in Madison, in the year 1840.

Q. 5.—State, from your knowledge and recollection, the invention and improvement of Mr. Hoyt, as disclosed to you in the year 1840—and state whether or not he made an improvement on his invention—the time when he made said improvement—and when he disclosed the same to you?

Ans.—The model then made was of four car wheels, and one cog wheel to work into the rack. That was geared on the axle of the driving wheels, which wheel received its power from a pinion on an intermediate shaft. The cog track laid between the rails. Some two weeks after I saw the model, I objected to it, on account of its getting out of gear, and breaking, on account of the unevenness of the track. A short time afterwards I saw him at the Depot, with the same model, at North Madison. He then said that he had obviated that difficulty. He then went on to describe the improvement—that he was going to have an intermediate cog-wheel, so constructed with bridgetrees or connecting rods as to play up and down and accommodate itself to the unevenness of track, to be held down to the rack by means of a lever, with weights or springs at the end of said lever. I had no understanding that it was to be more than a common locomotive, only that the intermediate or movable wheel conveyed the power from the pinion to the rack. This disclosure was made during the summer of 1840.

Q. 7th.—Did Hoyt so plainly disclose his invention or improvement that a mechanic could construct the machine and adapt it to use.

Ans.—A mechanic would, I think. I have no doubt a mechanic could have constructed and adapted it to use.

Q. 8.—State, if you know the fact, whether or not Hoyt has been engaged in improving, and perfecting his invention for use, ever since his discovery of said improvement. State whether you know Hoyt's circumstances, and if he has not made every exertion in his power to procure a patent for his invention.

Ans.—I do not know that he has been engaged ever since his disclosure to perfect his improvement. I know he has used a good deal of exertion to perfect his plans, put them into operation, and obtain a patent—and that he has made other improvements than those above described. Mr. Hoyt is poor in his circumstances. I know that he endeavored to obtain funds to enable him to obtain a patent.

Q. 9.--Was it known to the public that Hoyt had invented a new plan for the construction of Locomotives for ascending and descending inclined planes on Railroads—and has it not been generally talked about from the year 1840 to the present time.

Ans.—The improvement of Mr. Hoyt has been talked about a good deal, and from the year 1840 to the present time, has been generally known, so far as my knowledge extends about it.

James E. Patton, of lawful age, being next called to the stand, and being by me duly sworn according to law, deposeth and says:

Question 1st by Hoyt.—Are you acquainted with William Hoyt, and how long have you known him?

Ans.—I am acquainted with William Hoyt, and have known him for 22 or 23 years.

Q. by same—Did you ever see a model of said Hoyts? if so, describe it, and state when and where you saw it.

Ans.--I have seen a model of Mr. Hoyt's of a locomotive for planes of railroads. Between the years 1841 and 1842, I went to Mr. Hoyt's, and stayed all night there. After supper, Mr. Hoyt pulled a model out from under the bed. He (Hoyt) run it over the floor, and run it up on a rack. It had four car wheels and a frame, two cog wheels—a small one and a large one—the large one worked in a cog rack, and the little wheel worked into the big one. There was a lever attached to the big wheel. The track was unlevel when the lever worked up and down. The rack was in the centre.

Q. 3d, by same--Examine the exhibit marked "A" with the name of Gam'l Taylor, J. P., thereunto annexed, and say how the model compares with said exhibit?

Ans.—The movable wheel that worked into the rack, and the pinion wheel on the pinion shaft, that worked into the movable wheel are the same as the model of Hoyt's I saw. It had the upright pieces in the gearing of the lever shaft, and a single lever. The lever was connected with the wheel, and worked up and down, which was caused by the unevenness of the track. There was no other wheels inside the model than here described. I am by occupation a farmer. JAMES C. PATTON.

Subscribed and sworn to, before me, this 22d day of August, 1849.
GAM'L TAYLOR, J. P. [Seal.]

Part of Mr. Withers' Deposition.—Q. 3d, by Hoyt's attorney. Have you seen any other model of Hoyt's for the same improvement? If so, state when you saw the same—where you saw it—describe said model.

Ans.—I saw another model of Mr. Hoyt's as near as I can recollect in the year 1842. The said model was in my house. I kept a boarding house and stage office. Said model remained in my house from one to two months. It was a model with four car wheels, and two cog wheels inside the model. One was a small one, and the other a large one; the larger wheel worked into a cog rack that was laid in the centre of the track. Said wheel was operated upon by a lever connected with said cog wheel by a bridge tree or connecting rod. Said lever raised up or pressed down the wheel that worked into the rack, according to the unevenness of the track, as the car moved over the track the lever bobbed up and down when the track was uneven.

John Brough, Esq. alias the old Fox, and his emmissaries, W. N. Jackson, Esq., and A. Cathcart, have been busily engaged for the last year in attempting to pregudice the Public against my title to the improvement now in controversy between myself and Cathcart alias the R. R. Co, by circulating the report, that my model and specifications were taken from Cathcart's invention. In addition to the testimony that C's discovery was not made prior to the fall of 1844 or spring of 1845, and that my invention was actually discovered and the model made in 1840 to 1842, I give the depositions of Col. W. C. Bramwell as to the time when my specifications were drafted by him. Every citizen of Jefferson County knows who Col. Bramwell is, and what his report for integrity. The Col. testifies that he drew up my specification in the summer or fall of 1847, more than six months before Cathcart brought to Madison the locomotive constructed upon his pretended discovery. How then, fellow citizens, could I have stole C's invention unless indeed, C. voluntarily disclosed the same to me which is not pretended, but I forbear to make an argument of the same. Read the testimony for yourselves.

W. C. BRAMWELL'S DEPOSITION.—QUESTION 1st, *by Hoyt*—Are you acquainted with William Hoyt? Did you draw specifications for said Hoyt of an invention for the construction of locomotives for ascending and descending inclined planes in Rail Roads—If so state when you drew said specification?

ANS.—I am acquainted with William Hoyt's and drew for him specifications of said invention in the fall or summer of 1847. I drew said specifications from Hoyt's description of his invention.—Said invention was so fully and clearly explained to me that I understood it. Any mechanic skilled in the art to which it appertains have constructed a locomotive from the description given me upon the plan or principle of said invention and have adapted it to use.

Q. 2d *by same.*—Examine the drawings marked exhibit D. and state if it is a correct discription of Hoyt's invention for which you drew specifications as above stated?

ANS.—It is a correct description of said invention so far as the pinion wheel, the intermediate cog wheel that worked into the rack. the Bridgetrees or connecting rods attaching said intermediate cog wheel to the lever are concerned. Said lever is operated upon by weights or springs so as to adjust and accomodate said intermediate cog wheel to the uneveness of the track and further the said affiant saith not.

It is a fact worthy of notice, that almost every witness examined on behalf of Cathcart, were employees of the Railroad Company, and, as such, subject to removal by Mr. Brough, as President of the Road. Some of these witnesses were not only employees of the Railroad Company, but were, and still are, stockholders in said Company. W. N. Jackson, one of the chief witnesses of Cathcart. is not only the clerk of the Company, but is also a stockholder in the Road. Solon Bramwell stands in the same relation to the Road as Mr. Jackson, except that he is not a stockholder. being a clerk and ticket-master in the same. George Peterman, Benjamin McKeehan. Mr. Prindle. and Wm. Copeland, making up the majority of Cathcart's list of witnesses are all employees of said Company. And upon the testimony of these men—honest, no doubt, in their intentions, yet prejudiced against me, as they must be, by the relation which they sustain to the Railroad Company—was the controversy between Mr. C. and myself adjudged, by the Commissioner of Patents, notwithstanding that it was proven that the Railroad Company had an interest in the result of said controversy, by the contract existing between the Company and Cathcart.

As a sample of the spirit and manner in which George Peterman, Esq., the foreman of the machine shop of the Company, testified, I will here insert his deposition, and also the depositions of J. A. and W. P. Hendricks, contradicting him in a material point—viz: as to whether my model had or had not the lever attached to it, when exhibited at the office of J. A. Hendricks, in the city of Madison.

George Peterman—of lawful age and sound mind, being first duly sworn, deposes and says:

Question—*By Cathcart's Attorney.*—Are you acquainted with the improvement claimed by William Hoyt, for Locomotives on inclined planes? have you seen any models or drawings of the same? If so, state at what time and place—and describe said models or drawings, so far as the pinion and application to the track were concerned.

Answer.—I am acquainted with the improvement claimed by Mr. Hoyt, for locomotives on inclined planes. I saw a model of Mr. Hoyt's in Mr. Hendricks' law office, in this city, in the latter part of 1848, I think. I have just made a drawing representing the side and front view of the model. Mr. Hoyt called me into his office at the time, and showed me his model, and explained it to me. He caught hold of the crank and moved it backwards and forwards to show me the movement. I told him, then, that there was one thing wanting to it—that it did not equalize on the rack and rail—two levers ought to be put on it, with a spring or screw to hold it into the rack, after taking it out of the solid boxes at the side, and make a connection from the main driving wheel to the intermediate shaft, to suit the inequalities between the road and cog rack—otherwise it would be good for nothing.

His model had two pinions, one on the main driving wheel shaft of the car, and one on the intermediate shaft. The pinion and the intermediate shaft worked into the cog rack in the middle of the track.

Q. *by Cathcart's attorney.*—Was the cog wheel on said model that worked into the cog rack movable or stationery? Had it any perpendicular motion? Was there any gearing attached by lever or otherwise to put said wheel in or out of gear, and had it any means of accommodating itself to the uneveness of a Rail Road track? How would an engine built after that model operate on a track where the side rails were higher or lower than the cog rack on track?

Ans,--The cog wheel on said model that works into the cog rack was stationary on the intermediate shaft, and also on the levers. It had no perpendicular motion. There was no gearing attached by levers or otherwise to put said wheel in or out of gear. It had no means of accommodating itself to the unevenness of a railroad track. A locomotive constructed after that model if the side rails were higher than the cog track the cog wheel would not keep in gear with the cog track. If the side rails were lower than the cog rack it would be likely either to bend or break the intermediate shaft or throw the engine off the track.

I have introduced the testimony of Mr. Peterman to show how reckless the witnesses of my adversaries have been in their statements, and how variant is Peterman's testimony to that of Messrs. J. A. and W. P. Hendricks, sons of Ex-Governor Hendricks, who had a better opportunity to examine the model, and, therefore, here insert them.

John A. Handricks, of lawful age being first duly sworn according to law deposeth and saith:

Sometime in the summer of 1848 I was employed by Mr. Hoyt, as an attorney, to apply for a patent for an invention for the construction of locomotives for ascending and descending inclined planes on Rail Roads.

After my engagement, late in the summer or fall of said year, Mr. Hoyt brought to my office, situate one door north of the post office, on West st., Madison, Indiana, a model of his said invention or improvement, Said model was similar to the drawnings of the exhibit, D so far as the pinion wheel, intermediate cog-wheel Bridge trees. or connecting rods and levers, are concerned. It had, also, to my best recollection, the sliding wheel lock by the gearing of said model It had also attached to it on the front part of said model, machinery for sweeping the cog track, by means of revolving brooms. Said model is the only one ever brought to my office by Mr. Hoyt or any other person to my knowledge. The affidavit of Samuel Thomas in relation to Hoyts improvement, above referred to was carefully and fully explained to said Thomas before he subscribed or was sworn to the same, and further saith not.

Deposition of Wm. P. Hendricks,--Question *by Hoyt.*—Are you acquainted with Hoyt.

Ans --I am.

Q. 2d *by Hoyt.*—Did you, ever see a model of William Hoyt's for the construction of a locomotive for ascending and descending inclined planes on Railroads? If so, state when and where you saw it, and describe said model.

Ans.—I saw a model of said Hoyt's for the construction of locomotive for ascending and descending inclined planes of Railroads. I saw said model in the month of October 1848, at the office of John A. Hendricks, in this city. It was a wooden model, having six car wheels as I now recollect it. There were several cog wheels, one worked into a rack which was situated in the centre of the track, and raised up or pressed down, according to the uneveness of the track, by a lever which cog wheel was attached to the lever by a bridgetree or connecting rods. This is the oly model I ever saw of the kind. I have been in said office ever since the first of June or July 1848, engaged in the study of Law. I was staying in said office at the time Hoyt employed John A. Hendricks as his attorney in this case to Hoyt's fetching his model to said cffice. At the time I saw said model, there was a weight on said lever, showing the principle on which it operates, in accommodating the intermediate cog wheel to the unevenness of the track. This is the only model of any kind brought to or exhibited at said office since I have been there; and further this deponent saith not.

Part of the Cross-Examination of Mr. Jackson.—Question—by Hoyt's Attorney.—You say that in or after June, 1848, you saw Mr. Hoyt's model for the construction of a locomotive for ascending and descending inclined planes, on Railroads. Describe that model and explain wherein it differed from Mr. Cathcart's invention.

Ans.—I saw the model of Mr. Hoyt but a very short time, and had not opportunity for examination—but observed a part of it was new work, and think that part related to the movable pinion. Mr. Hoyt put the model on the cars, immediately, as the train was started. If that new work did make the pinion a movable and self-adjustinng one, in that, it was similar to Mr. Cathcart's, but in little else, except the driving wheels and other parts necessary to make up any engine.

Q.—by Same.—Can you not, from the examination you gave of Mr. Hoyt's model, in or after June, 1848, describe said model? If so, describe it as minutely as possible.

Ans.—I think it had two pairs of drivers, with a pinion working into a rack in the center of the track, which pinion, I think, was then movable, and had recently been made such.

Q.—How do you know that the movable pinion had been recently made so? Do you form your opinion from the appearance of the work? If so, state how you distinguish between inventions recently made and those of older date.

Ans. The work looked new.

Q. Might not the invention have been discovered years ago, and the model been recently made?

Ans. I should think so.

Q. By Cathcart's Attorney.—In what particular, as you understood it, was the model of Mr. Hoyt altered?

Ans. It was altered to make the pinion movable. As I had heard the model described all along, the pinion was stationary, and in this model, he showed me, it was movable, and the movable part was new.

Q.---By Hoyt's Attorney.---Had the Madison and Indianapolis Railroad Company any contract with Andrew Cathcart in reference to the locomotive now in use on the inclined plane of said Road? If so, state what that contract was.

Ans. They have a contract with Mr. Cathcart to give him $1000 per year, for his services on the plane, and $6,000 in 1853, if his experiment is successful in taking up and letting down the proposed quantity of freight on the plane, which $6000 is contingent upon his procuring a Patent, and conveying the right to the Company.

Here may be seen the interest of the Railroad Company to sustain Cathcart. If C. does not succeed, the Company will have to make a new contract with me, and also pay damages for the use of my invention. The invention, having been tried, proves itself to be worth more than was supposed before its operation on the plane was tried, and hence the Company are afraid, if I succeed, they will have to pay something like a fair value for the improvement.

The reader will perceive that Mr. Jackson who is Principal clerk, stockholder and Director of the Railroad Conmpany has testified that the movable wheel in the model (the only important matter in controversy.) when he examined it the next morning after it was examined by Peterman, appeared to have been newly made and signifying it to have been fitted to an old model to which I oppose the following testimony of Mr. Shrewsbury, who is a highly respectable mechanic and disinterested in the matter.

STATE OF INDIANA, } To-wit
Jefferson County, }

Personally appeared before me a justice of the peace in and for said county, Irvin Shrewsbury, and made oath, according to law, that in the summer or fall of 1848, I assisted Mr. William Hoyt in making his model in my shop, at Dupont, Indiana, for the construction of a locomotive for ascending and descending inclined planes on Rail Roads, and that I did his Blacksmith work for him. This model had four car wheels placed in a frame. There were several cog wheels inside of said frame two of them were so arranged as to propel the locomotive up the plane. The pinion wheel to which the pitman was attached, worked in a larger wheel This larger wheel mashed in a cog rack placed in the centre of the track, and was fastened on a shaft—said shaft resting on bridge trees or connexion rods, and was pressed down into the cog rack by means of a lever with weights so that this intermediate cog wheel would adjust itself to the uneveness of the track. I further state that every part of this model was made new at the time and that said Hoyt took it to Madison, in said county, after he had it finished it to exhibit there. He afterwards brought it back to Dupont. In March, 1849, said Hoyt started with this same model to the city of Washington to obtain a patent, without any alteration on said model whatever,

IRVIN SHREWSBURY.

Sworn and subscribed to, before me, this 13th day of Nov 1849.

THOMAS TROUSDAIL, J. P.

Augustus B. Stoughton, a witness for plaintiff, being first sworn, tesiified as follows:

Q.—What is your present occupation?

ANS.—Machinist of the Patent Office.

Q. 2.—What time were you appointed to said office?

ANS:—July 1st, 1848.

Q. 3.—Were you a machinist when William Hoyt's application for a patent for his improved locomotive for ascending inclined planes was examined, and the patent granted.

Ans.—I was.

Q. 4.—Do you know whether any modifications have been made to or in addition to the model of William Hoyt's locomotive for ascending and descending inclined planes since it was deposited in the Patent Office, and if so, what was the nature of those changes, and at what time were they made!

Ans.—There were additions made, to-wit: a lever and weight to hold the spur wheel in gear with the rack. These additions were made during the progress of the examination.

Q. 5. Why was not Mr. Cathcart's model carried up when Mr Hoyt's application was before the examiner!

Ans. Because it was not credited on the books of the office.

Mr. Stoughton cross-examined by Mr. Elliott. Q. 1. Was Cathcart's application considered complete anterior to the examination of Hoyt's application!

Ans. It was complete, inasmuch as everything necessary to render it complete was in the office, owing to neglect of the clerks it failed to get its proper direction.

Q. 2. Were not the alterations in the model made by the order of the examiner, to make the model agree with the drawings!

Ans. I do not know that they were.

Q. 3. Was there any material alteration in the essential feature, namely, the rising and falling pinion!

Ans. There was the addition of a lever and weight to throw the spur wheel into gear and keep it there.

Q. 4. Did not the drawings show the lever and weight, just referred to!

Ans. I do not recollect to have seen the drawing.

Q. 5. Who ordered the alterations in the model!

Ans. I do not know; and further this deponent saith not.

A. B. STOUGHTON.

The above testimony was taken at the City of Washington in my absence. and the parties rely much upon the reputation of the witness for his offiicial standing and his experience as a machinist. request that his deposition may be critically reviewed, by which it will appeal that the lever and weights were added to the model by Hoyt after it was deposited in the Patent office and during the progress of the examination, when Mr Jackson, another of their witness, testafies that the improvement above mentioned had been newly attached when he saw it in Madison, Indiana, previous to my taking the model to Washington City. Strange consistency! I now refer the public to the testimony of Wm P. Elliot Esq, of the Patent office who certainly is entitled to as much distinction of character as Mr Stoughton, he having long acted as draftsman and Patent agent, and many years official surveyor of Washington City, accompanied with the testimony of A. E. H. Johnson, draughsman, and J. B. Woodruff, model maker. and leave the public to judge of the credit due to Mr. Stoughton's testimony.

We, the subscribers, solemnly declare that we have examined Mr. William Hoyt's model of a locomotive for ascending and descending inclined planes of steep grades, by rack and pinion, now in the Patent Office, and for which Letters Patent were granted to him on the seventeenth day of April, A. D. 1849, and found it to be substantially the same as when first exhibited in the City of Washington, at the office of Wm. P. Elliott, Patent Attorney, and at the United States Patent Office, and that the lever for raising and lowering the intermediate cog wheel that matches into the rack, formed a part of the combination in the said model.

City of Washington, Sept. 21. 1849,

WM. P. ELLIOT,
A. E. H. JOHNSON,
J. B. WOODRUFF.

COUNY OF WASHINGTON, }
District of Columbia, } SS.

On this twenty first day of September A. D. 1849, personally appeared before the subscriber, a Justice of the Peace in and for the said County, Wm. P. Elliot, solicitor for Patents, Albert E. H. Johnson, Draughtsman, and J. B. Woodruff, Model Maker, and made solemn oath to the truth of the above statement.

LUND WASHINGTON J. P. [Seal.]

WASHINGTON CITY Oct. 1st 1849.

This is to certify, that, sometime in the spring or summer of 1840, William Hoyt brought to my shop, in this city, a model for a a locomotive to ascend and and descend inclined planes on Rail roads, and that said Hoyt repaired the same at my shop. I can say from the best of my recollection and belief that it had two wheels, one larger than the other, and that the larger one worked in a cog rack, and was operated upon by a lever and weights to press it down to the uneveness of the track.

W. LITTLE.

DISTRICT OF COLUMBIA, }
County of Washington, } To-wit.

Personally appeared before me, the subscriber, a justice of the peace for the county aforesaid Warren Little, and subscribed his name to, and made oath in due form, that the facts set forth and contained in the foregoing certificates are true as stated, to the best of his knoweldge and belief.

Given under my hand and seal, this first day of Oct., 1849.

C. ASHFORD, J. P. [Seal.]

WASHINGTON, Oct. 3, 1849.

MR. WM. HOYT:—*Sir:* At your request, I have carefully examined the papers placed by you in my hands, which you say are true copies of the testimonials taken on both sides of the matter of interference before the patent office between you and Andrew Cathcart, both claiming a device for ascending and descending inclined planes on railroads. I understand that you both claim substantially the same device, which is a mechanical combination by which the wheel operating in the rack or middle rail, is adapted to the inequalities which it may encounter. I therefore do not go into an examination of the nature or character of the two devices, assuming that they are substantially identical, and interfere, but consider merely the fact of priority of invention confining my investigation to the question, of priority of privilege between you and Mr. Cathcart.

I have carefully examined the testimony, and have come to the conclusion that you are the original and first inventor.

It appears from the testimony, that you invented the device, and produced it in the form of a model between 1840 and 1842, whereas Mr. Cathcart did not, according to the testimony presented by him, invent it before the latter part of 1844 or early in 1845. I think no other conclusion can be arrived at without throwing out entirely the testimony of three or four witnesses who stand a wholly unimpeached.

In expressing the opinion that the testimony, carefully considered, leads to this result, I do not of course design or wish to reflect upon any officer of the Government who has passed upon your case. for I have doubt that all who have had anything to do with it, have desired to do you justice. I express only my own candid conviction after a careful examination of the testimony, regarding the question merely as one of fact.

I am, respectfully, your obedient servant,

EDMUND BURKE.

Vernon, Jennings County, Indiana, ss.

Horace Bacon, being duly sworn, on his oath saith, that at some time in or between the years 1840 and 1842, he helped William Hoyt make a model, at his house, near Dupont, of his improved Locomotive for ascending and descening inclined plains on Railroads. Said model had four driving car wheels placed on a frame; there were also two cog wheels; the driving pinion worked into the large cog wheel. and that wheel into a cog rack, in the center of the track. This wheel rested on two bridge trees or connecting rods, so arranged as to conform to the unevenness of the track, to which they were held by means of a lever with weights or by springs. HORACE BACON.

Sworn to and subscribed before me, this 2d day of February, 1850. PHILANDER L. BASNETT, J. P. [Seal.]

Further, fellow-citizens, I have to say that the controversy between Cathcart and myself was decided by Henry B. Renwick, a Scotchman, and brother to the Renwick who was agent for Cathcart during this whole controversy.

Thomas Ewbank, Esq., an Englishman, is nominally the Commissioner of Patents, while Henry B. Renwick, chief Examiner of models in the Patent Office is the real Commissioner. My reasons for stating that Henry B. Renwick decided the controversy between Cathcart and myself are these:

The testimony of A. B. Stoughton, and others, had been taken at Washington City, in my absence, and I applied to the Commissioner of Patents to continue the hearing of the case, in order to cross-examine the witnesses. He replied that he would consult Mr. Renwick. He rang his bell, and Mr. R. made his appearance. Mr. Ewbank made known to him the application I had made for a continuance of my case, in order to cross-examine witnesses whose depositions had been taken in my absence. Mr. R. said—"The case cannot be continued;" Mr. Ewbank echoed—"The case cannot be continued." One week afterwards, I called and asked our English Commissioner, Mr. Ewbank, when my case would be decided. He replied he did not know, but would consult Mr. Renwick. He rang the bell, and Mr. R. made his appearance, whereupon, Mr. E. said to Mr. R.—"When will you decide Mr. Hoyt's case." Mr. R. replied—"this afternoon." Mr. Ewbank then said to me—"Your case will be decided this afternoon." Accordingly, in the afternoon of the same day, I was informed that a patent would be issued to Cathcart for the same invention patented by me, in April last. Some days afterwards, I filed a petition for a new hearing of the case, setting forth that, because of an unavoidable accident occurring—to-wit: the cars running off the track, on the railroad between Cincinnati and Sandusky City, thereby causing me to lose two days' time, I had been unable to reach Washington City in time to cross-axamine witnesses whose depositions had been taken in my absence. Upon making this application, Mr. Ewbank said he would consult Mr. Renwick. Mr. R. was called in, and the petition was presented to him—to which he replied—"We cannot grant a new hearing of the case." Mr. Ewbank echoed, "We cannot grant a new hearing of the case." So you see, fellow-citizens, the brother to Cathcart's agent, and a brother Scotchman, actually decided the controversy between Cathcart and myself.

It seems that Mr. Brough, the President of the Railroad, for the purpose of diverting the public from a view of the interest which the Railroad Company has in this controversy, published a card in the Indiana State Sentinel, dated Jan. 4, 1850, over his signature, as "*of Counsel for Cathcart.*" By this device, he attempts to establish the fact that the untiring energies of himself and other eminent servants of the Company, and the unsparing expenditure of time and money, have been appropriated as "of Counsel for Cathcart." It is true that the name of Cathcart must be employed in the investigation, and so must the name of Jonh Doe, or some other one as senseless. be used, as casual ejector, in a fictitious action for the recovery of possession—yet, he cannot conceal from those acquainted with the facts in this case. that he is "of Counsel" for the Company of which he is chief, and armed with all the influence and talents which money can purchase, for the promotion of her wicked designs.

The gentleman "of counsel for Mr. Cathcart" alludes, in his card, to my late circular, in which he says, "He seeks to play the demagogue, by creating a local and sectional sympathy for himself," and that "it is most certainly an indication of a weak cause." I can inform him that my injury which he seeks is not "local and sectional," but limited only by the boundaries of our Union, and the justice he would pervert has something more than a "local habitation a name." The excitement which may have been induced, is not local, but general as the knowedge of the facts, and is the natural result of outraged rights, of the indomitable power of wealth over the weakness of poverty, and the combination of unscrupulous and pensioned agents over unaided helplessness. Feeble as I am in pecuniary resources, I have left me a confidence in the power of the law, which a salaried agent cannot thwart, and in the integrity of a jury which their influence cannot reach, nor their patronage corrupt. With a fixed purpose to an immediate resort to a legal tribunal for redress, and the establishment of my rights upon an indisputable basis, I ask and kindly admonish my fellow-citizens to await its decision, before they negotiate with Mr. Cathcart for any presumptive right to the foregoing invention which he may possess, and in the meantime, I invite all who may have any inerest in the subject matter refered to above, to address me, as formerly, at my residence, at Dupont, Indiana.

DUPONT, February 16th, 1850 WILLIAM HOYT.

www.ingramcontent.com/pod-product-compliance
Lightning Source LLC
LaVergne TN
LVHW020636110826
845149LV00004B/1230

* 9 7 8 1 4 1 8 1 9 1 1 7 7 *